My Redefined American Dream

A Workbook Compendium to "Money Shackles"

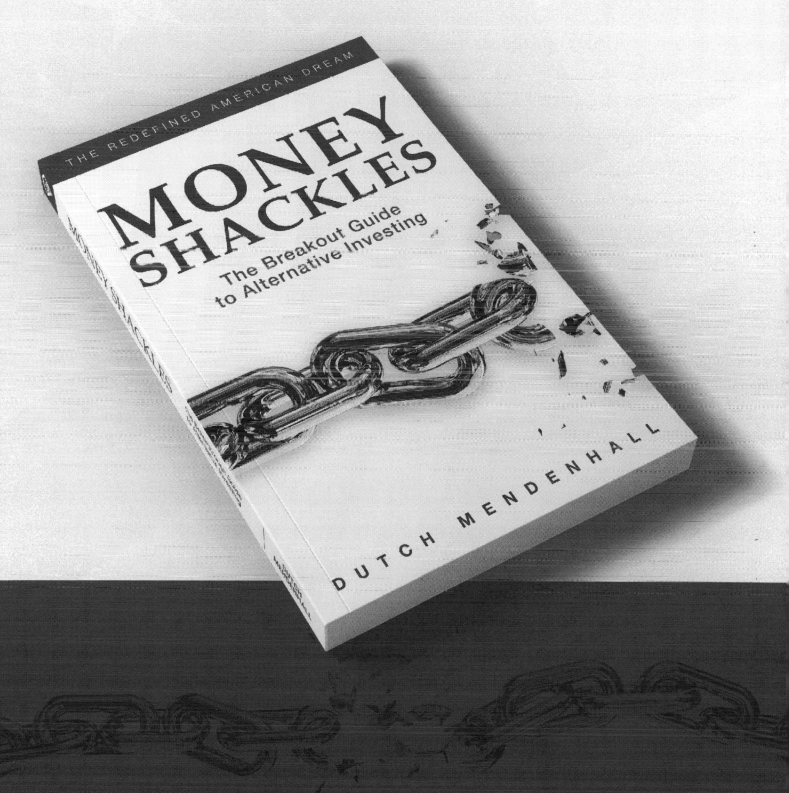

My Redefined American Dream
A Workbook Compendium to "Money Shackles"

The workbook is a practical guide based on "Money Shackles: The Breakout Guide to Alternative Investing" that addresses the issue of financial vulnerability experienced by many Americans.

Readers will learn about their money personality, diversification, and alternative investing methods, such as fractional ownership.

With exercises and activities, the workbook offers a hands-on approach to financial education and empowers readers to take control of their financial future.

CH1 The Reality of Financial Vulnerability

Activation Prompt	Lessons from Chapter 1
• Define where you are currently and your vision of the American Dream. • Take actionable steps by creating a personal financial framework. • Evaluate your financial freedom.	• Four Freedom Principles • Building Blocks • Freedom Chart

Exercise 1

This exercise is fun because it allows you to craft a future vision of your life. I encourage you to suspend your doubts and objections based on your past or present. This is your opportunity to dream about what you want your life to be like.

In "My American Dream" life...

1. I am (relationship status)? Example: I am happily married for 30 years and am madly in love with my spouse. We have 3 grown children (who are thriving) and 4 grandchildren. We spend much time with family sowing into their lives.

_____

_____

_____

2. I am (health status)? Example: I am fit and healthy. I exercise daily and eat a clean, organic-based, heart, gut, and brain-healthy diet. My health status is carefully monitored by a team of wholistic-oriented health care professionals. I am proactive in the maintenance of my body.

_____

_____

_____

3. I am (spiritual status)? Example: I am devoted to my faith as a Christian. My daily disciplines include prayer, meditation, reading/studying, and worship. My spouse and I are actively serving the needy in our community through our church's outreach ministries. We devote 2 weeks per year to mission trips and take our entire family. We live on 50% of our income and donate 50% to impacting those in need.

_____

_____

_____

4. I am (financial status)? Example: I am financially free. Our net worth is 20M. Our passive and residual income is 40K per month. We live on 20K and give the other 40K away charitability. Our dream home is paid off, we have no debt, and we pay off our credit cards monthly. We have 2 years of living expenses in a liquid account, earning a modest return. Our investments are diversified into several risk buckets and have continually exceeded the market and inflation substantially. Our 20K per month far exceeds our monthly expenses. We reinvest the difference.

_____

_____

_____

5. I am (work status)? Example: I own 2 businesses and spend 2 hours/week meeting with each company's CEO, COO, and CFO. I act in a purely advisory capacity. I serve on the board of two charities, which requires 2 hours (1 for each) per week in virtual meetings and in-person once per quarter for a half day. I volunteer 2 mornings each week to feed the homeless through my church.

_____

_____

_____

Closing the Gap – Let's consider where we are currently at in the areas above and list 5 key priorities that will begin the process of building your "American Dream". What priorities will move you powerfully toward achieving your dream when compounded over time?

My 5 Key Priorities

1. _____

2. _____

3. _____

4. _____

5. _____

Additional Notes:

Exercise 2

This exercise will awaken your achievement muscles in gaining mastery over your financial future.

My Present Financial Profile

1. My yearly household income:
   - Gross
   - Net
2. My monthly spendable income:
3. My total monthly expenses:
4. My monthly savings:
5. My total asset worth (value of what you own):
6. My total debt (amount of what you owe):
7. My net worth (subtract what you owe from what you own):

How can I improve my (our) financial profile?

1. I can add more income by (check each one you can do):
   - ☐ Better Job
   - ☐ Ask for a Raise
   - ☐ Second Job
   - ☐ Passive Investment
   - ☐ Other

2. I can reduce expenses by (check each one you can do):
   - ☐ Set and keep a budget below my income.
   - ☐ Reasonably reducing my entertainment spending.
   - ☐ Eating out less often.
   - ☐ Paying off Credit Cards every month.
   - ☐ Stopping impulse buying.
   - ☐ Shop my insurance coverage yearly.
   - ☐ Performing proactive maintenance on my house.

3. I commit to saving _____ every month.

Exercise 3

Commitment Plan – I am committed to...

1. Reviewing my budget (income and expenses) every month/week on _____ (day or date).

2. Increasing my monthly savings to _____ (amount) by _____ (date).

3. Having a reserve for emergencies of _____ (amount) by _____ (date).

4. Investing _____ (amount) toward passive income by _____ (date).

5. I will read 1 book, listen to 1 podcast, or read one article every _____ on financial education.

Additional Notes:

CH2

Your Redefined American Dream Starts Coming True Today

Activation Prompt	Lessons from Chapter 2
• Define your focal point by making choices that lead to your reinvention. • Establish your starting point and prioritize your money and risk buckets. • Identify and list the risks and changes that will have you step out of your comfort zone.	• Financial Decision Tree • Money Buckets • Risk Buckets

Exercise 1

Mindset: My journey has defined me. The battles I endured were designed to prepare me for greater things.

The battles that led me to where I am today.

_____

_____

_____

_____

What I learned from them.

_____

_____

_____

_____

Areas I want to "Pivot" or "Reinvent" myself to make major life changes and alter my trajectory in life.

Example: I want to identify, research, and plan in my career, education, location, relationships, passions, health, or personal development.

_____

_____

_____

The "Critical Decisions" or "Strategies" I make today are to help me move forward in managing goals and opportunities.

Example: I will specifically act and begin a debt reduction program, increase my financial IQ, invest in myself, and start a monthly savings/ investment plan.

_____

_____

_____

Exercise 2

Begin with the end in mind!

In Chapter 1: Exercise #1, you crafted your "Redefined American Dream". In this exercise, you must choose the path/focal point you want to take to reach it. You want to focus on starting a business or scaling your current business. Maybe you want to become a real estate investor or day trade in the stock market. Many of you will join the RADD Inner Circle and Invest with our team of specialists.

My Focal Point forward is _____

In what way does this focal point decision excite you? Write your feeling down here and how you will work to achieve them.

_____

_____

_____

Evaluate your Starting Point

1. What resources do you have available? What areas do you need to improve upon? This is a review from Chapter 1: Exercises #2 and #3.

    ☐ Income

    ☐ Budget and Reducing Living Costs
    (This will mean items where you can reduce and are unimportant to you or your goals and not areas that will keep you happy, like buying a brand drink compared to the in-house store brand.)

    ☐ Increase Savings and Emergency Reserve

    ☐ Investments

    ☐ Continuing Financial Education

    _____

    _____

2. Now divide your financial resources into "money buckets" based on their intended use. For example, you may have a bucket for savings, investing in your chosen path/focal point, and paying off debt. Determine how much money you can allocate to each bucket and prioritize them based on their importance in achieving your goal.

3. Let's consider your risk tolerance. How much risk are you comfortable pursuing your chosen path/focal point? This will be the focus of the next exercise.

☐ high-risk/high-reward

1	2	3	4	5	6	7	8	9	10

least likely   most likely

☐ high-risk/low-reward

1	2	3	4	5	6	7	8	9	10

least likely   most likely

☐ low-risk/high-reward

1	2	3	4	5	6	7	8	9	10

least likely   most likely

☐ low-risk/low-reward

1	2	3	4	5	6	7	8	9	10

least likely   most likely

☐ moderate-risk investments

1	2	3	4	5	6	7	8	9	10

least likely   most likely

Now look at how you rated the risks, and think about how much each one would be in a piece of pie, or out of 100%. There are five portions, about 20% each. If you rated it below 5, it may be 0-10%. If you rated it above 5, it may be 10-20%.

☐ high-risk/high-reward   _____

☐ high-risk/low-reward   _____

☐ low-risk/high-reward   _____

☐ low-risk/low-reward   _____

☐ moderate-risk investments   _____

Total: **100%**

Exercise 3

Now that you've identified your risk tolerance, let's dive deeper into your risk buckets.

You can use the risk buckets to determine which types of investments align with your comfort level. Remember that your risk buckets are subject to how much you want to invest and can change over time. However, consider each one carefully and how it will help with your goals, even if it requires stepping outside your comfort zone.

After reviewing the pros and cons of each alternative investment, check which ones you will ultimately consider investing in for each of your risk buckets.

1. high-risk/high-reward	**Pros**	**Cons**
☐ Private Equity		
☐ Commodities		
☐ Futures		

2. high-risk/low-reward

☐ Penny Stocks

	Pros	Cons
☐ Rental Properties		

☐ Start-Up Investments

3. low-risk/high-reward

☐ REITs

☐ Peer-to-Peer Lending

☐ Crowdfunding

4. low-risk/low-reward

☐ Savings Bonds

	Pros	Cons
☐ High-Yields Savings Accounts		

5. moderate-risk investments

	Pros	Cons
☐ Money Market Accounts		
☐ Private Debt (or Infrastructure Projects)		
☐ Arts and Collectibles		
☐ Corporate Bonds		

Now let's make the picture clear, write the type of investment that interested you the most for each risk bucket. Do you feel confident about your next action, and will you research each investment type more in-depth?

Additional Notes:

CH3

Assessing Your Money Personality

Activation Prompt	Lessons from Chapter 3
• Reflect on your money personality and your personalities' strengths.	• Five Money Personalities
• Strategize how to attain your financial goals.	• An Investor's Important Steps
• Identify any beliefs or habits that may hinder your financial success.	• Ten Costly Mistakes

Exercise 1

Start by taking this free test at **https://5moneypersonalities.com** (Additional Money Tests: **https://fullbalance.co.nz/money-quiz-saving-money-feelings-about** and **https://moneycoachinginstitute.com/money-type-quiz/**).
After reviewing your results, do the following:

List your Primary and Secondary Money Personality type.

_____

_____

_____

How can this information help you make better money decisions?

Primary: _____

_____

_____

_____

Secondary: _____

_____

_____

_____

My action plan moving forward is:

_____

_____

_____

Money Shackles

Exercise 2

Have you struggled with...   Action, I'll take to correct...

☐ Overspending

_____

_____

_____

☐ Debt

_____

_____

_____

☐ Financial Insecurity

_____

_____

_____

☐ Negative Beliefs Towards Money

_____

_____

_____

☐ Fear of a Scarcity of Money

_____

_____

_____

☐ Money being Inherently Evil

_____

_____

_____

Based on these assumptions, what steps as an investor for your personality, can you take, and what does that look like?

Primary: _____

1. Due Diligence

2. Investment Vehicle Education

3. Leverage Others' Experiences

4. Leverage Others' Work

5. Don't Let the Past Hold You Back From Success

Secondary: _____

1. Due Diligence

2. Investment Vehicle Education

3. Leverage Others' Experiences

4. Leverage Others' Work

5. Don't Let the Past Hold You Back From Success

Exercise 3

What is your Money Story?

Briefly write out your history with money. Include how your parents or family influenced your money relationship and any unhealthy patterns in your life.

_____

_____

_____

_____

_____

Write out your action on how you will address any unhealthy issues. (Example: Take a financial planning/education course, seek professional help, etc.)

_____

_____

_____

_____

_____

Understanding your money story (the unhealthy patterns you identified and your money personality results), list your action plan for breaking free of your shackles. Using positive, affirming language will accelerate you past the prior stumbling blocks that worked against you in the past. (Example: I take full responsibility for my financial future and will actively save and invest wisely 10% of my income every month)

_____

_____

_____

_____

_____

Additional Notes:

Reframing Debt and Borrowing

Activation Prompt	Lessons from Chapter 4
• Look at your changing attitudes towards debt and borrowing. • Identify the resources and strategies that best fit your needs. • Discuss the compounding effect on your capital growth and financial freedom.	• Personal Finance Information • Alternative Approach to Debt • Two Wealth Mindsets

Exercise 1

Describe how debt has impacted your life and how you feel about it.

How did your parents or family view debt throughout your life?

_____

_____

_____

How did your friends, peers, and mentors view debt throught your life?

_____

_____

_____

Thus, how did you view debt and borrowing, even a pencil or game from a classmate, as a kid and throughout high school?

_____

_____

_____

How has this changed as you entered adulthood, and what were the biggest moments that affected how you viewed money?

_____

_____

_____

If you're close to retirement age, detail how you view debt and borrowing from when you were younger, and what do you teach to the younger generations?

_____

_____

_____

Exercise 2

Create your debt strategy below:

Unsecured Debt – Debt not backed by an asset such as a home or car.

Debt I Will Eliminate, Reduce, or Leverage	Resources	My Action Plan
☐ Medical Bills	_____	_____
	_____	_____
	_____	_____
☐ Personal Loans	_____	_____
	_____	_____
	_____	_____
☐ Student Loans	_____	_____
	_____	_____
	_____	_____

Revolving Debt – can be secured or unsecured.

Debt I Will Eliminate, Reduce, or Leverage

☐ Credit Cards	_____	_____
	_____	_____
☐ Lines of Credit	_____	_____
	_____	_____

	Resources	My Action Plan
☐ HELOC	_____	_____
	_____	_____
	_____	_____

Installment Debt – a loan that provides a lump-sum amount of money as loan starts.

Debt I Will Eliminate, Reduce, or Leverage	Resources	My Action Plan
☐ Auto Loan	_____	_____
	_____	_____
	_____	_____
☐ Mortgage Loan	_____	_____
	_____	_____
	_____	_____
☐ Business Loan	_____	_____
	_____	_____
	_____	_____

What's the best way to utilize debt and what will that look like for you?

_____

_____

_____

_____

_____

Exercise 3

Let's take a moment and visualize the future. You know what unhealthy habits prevent you from utilizing debt to expand your earning potential and, more specifically, what steps to take with each specific type of debt. You have your resources and action plans from Exercise #2.

What would the compounding effect on your capital growth look like if you implemented it and found a clear path[1] to your financial freedom?

[1]Alance, AB. 2023. Maze Generator. Retrieved from **https://mazegenerator.net/**.

Money Shackles

Additional Notes:

CH5

Getting Started with Alternative Investing

Activation Prompt	Lessons from Chapter 5

- Identify different alternative investment vehicles.

- Apply research to different vehicles' credibility and risks.

- Discuss how these vehicles could or could not be implemented by reflecting on your goals.

- The JOBS Act

- The RAD Keys

- Develop an Alternative Mindset

Exercise 1

Which one is an alternative investment vehicle:

	Alternative	Traditional
Alternative	☐	☐
Traditional	☐	☐
Exchange Traded Funds (ETFs)	☐	☐
Farms and Ranches	☐	☐
US Treasury Bonds	☐	☐
Timber	☐	☐
Rare Books	☐	☐
Dividend Stocks	☐	☐
Angel Investing	☐	☐
Renewable Energy	☐	☐
Video Game Rights	☐	☐
Savings Account	☐	☐
Social Impact Bonds	☐	☐

Which investment vehicle has potentially seen an increase in funding opportunities, after the passing of the JOBS Act of 2012. List only five below.

1. _____

2. _____

3. _____

4. _____

5. _____

Exercise 2

Let's dive deeper into the credibility and risks of Private Equity and Growth Equity investments.

First, define in 3 words or less what Private Equity is: _____

_____

_____

Next, define in 3 words or less what Growth Equity is: _____

_____

_____

Pick from the list below one of the Growth Equity companies:

- Accel Partners (**https://www.accel.com/**)

- Sequoia Capital (**https://www.sequoiacap.com/**)

- General Atlantic (**https://www.generalatlantic.com/**)

- Norwest Venture Partners (**https://www.nvp.com/**)

- ICONIQ Capital (**https://www.iconiqcapital.com/**)

Use the RAD Keys to fill out the table below to determine if the company you picked aligns with your financial goals to achieve your American Dream. If it doesn't, that's okay. This learning process ensures you're asking the right questions about what investment works for you.

Business Name:		
CEO (Who)	Niche (What)	Began (When and Where)
The RAD Keys	(Why or Options)	(How or Success Rate)
Understand the founder's story and find a successful track record.		
Invest in real businesses, not just good ideas.		
Is it clear whether the business offers a real product?		
What is the business model for profitability?		
Does the business have existing revenue?		
Do they know their current profit margins per product?		
Is there a specific, measurable timeline for the company's growth?		
Does business exist in regulated industries?		
What are the biggest obstacles to success? Does the business have a plan for overcoming obstacles?		
What type of impact does the business have in the world?		

Review the other different types of alternative investments with each asset class, then research on your own. Use the table above to help organize your thoughts.

Exercise 3

Document your journey of how your mindset has changed over time.

1. What did you think when you were 18 years old? Were you finding personal development programs, setting future goals, and planning to protect your wealth?

_____

_____

_____

2. What did you think of wealth before you started alternative investing? Was a portion of your income already going toward savings and investments?

_____

_____

_____

3. When you first started investing and needed more education or experience, how did your views change, and what mishaps did you encounter?

_____

_____

_____

4. After a while, how did your views change? Were you managing your cash flow by compounding and cycling money for incoming capital to exceed your expenses?

_____

_____

_____

5. After reviewing the book and these exercises, has your mindset changed again, and where do you think your purpose is or will be in 10 years?

_____

_____

After understanding your journey, the skills needed, and how certain influences can affect decision-making. Imagine what a portfolio will look like for the scenarios below.

Investor A	Investor B	Investor C
The Adventurous Entrepreneur Young and ambitious, and recently sold his startup for significant money. He is looking for high-growth investments to continue building his wealth.	The Cautious Retiree A retired teacher who has a modest pension and savings. She is risk-averse and wants to preserve her capital while generating a reliable income stream.	The Socially Responsible Millennial A young professional passionate about social and environmental issues. She wants to invest her money in companies that have a positive impact.
Risk-Taker and Flyer	Security-Seeker and Saver	Saver and Spender
high risk-high reward	low risk-high reward	moderate-risk

1. Which of the following investments would be most suitable for Investor C?
    a. Venture Capital
    b. Angel Investing
    c. Crowdfunding

2. Which of the following investments would be most suitable for Investor B?
    a. REITs
    b. Private Equity
    c. Social Impact Bonds (SIBs)

3. Which of the following investments would be most suitable for Investor A?
    a. Cryptocurrencies
    b. Art and Collectibles
    c. Renewable Energy Projects

4. Notice that all of the answers in #1-3 will fit one investor profile. The other responses to each question will fit the other investors' profiles provided. This creates a diversified portfolio for each investor profile with 3 investment options.

What percentage of their capital should go to the following money buckets, and what's missing from each investment portfolio?

Investor A

Living Costs _____
Savings _____
Debt _____
Misc. Buckets _____

Investment:
Venture Capital _____
Private Equity _____
Cryptocurrencies _____

= 100%

Investor B

Living Costs _____
Savings _____
Debt _____
Misc. Buckets _____

Investment:
Angel Investing _____
REITs _____
Art/Collectibles _____

= 100%

Investor C

Living Costs _____
Savings _____
Debt _____
Misc. Buckets _____

Investment:
Crowdfunding _____
SIBs _____
Renewable Energy _____

= 100%

5. The following companies are from a similar asset class. Which one would Investor A specifically be interested in?

   a. Company A: This venture capital firm is known for investing in well-established companies with a proven track record. They prioritize stability, rarely invest in startups, and prefer traditional industries.

   b. Company B: This venture capital firm takes a cautious approach, preferring to invest in stable, established businesses with consistent cash flows. They are not interested in cryptocurrency or unproven startups.

   c. Company C: This venture capital firm specializes in high-growth investments and has a strong record of backing successful startups. They willingly take risks in innovative technologies and emerging industries.

6. The following companies are from a similar asset class. Which one would Investor B specifically be interested in?

   a. Company A: This REIT invests in high-growth real estate assets like hotels, resorts, and commercial properties. They are willing to take risks to achieve high returns.

b. Company B: This REIT prioritizes generating a reliable income stream by investing in stable, income-producing real estate assets such as apartment buildings, office parks, and shopping centers.

c. Company C: This REIT invests in high-yield, high-risk real estates assets such as distressed properties and speculative developments.

7. The following companies are from a similar asset class. Which one would Investor C specifically be interested in?

a. Company A: This crowdfunding platform focuses solely on maximizing returns for investors without regard for social or environmental impact. They prioritize profitability in their investments.

b. Company B: This crowdfunding platform funds high-risk ventures, such as early-stage startups or speculative projects. They may not have a proven track record or a clear plan for community impacts.

c. Company C: This crowdfunding platform connects investors with companies with a positive social or environmental impact. They actively seek out opportunities for positive change.

Reflect: After reading the chapter and completing the exercises, do you feel you understand the importance of an Alternative Investment Mindset?

Additional Notes:

Choosing Fractional Ownership

Activation Prompt	Lessons from Chapter 6
• List different types of fractional ownership investments.	• Obstacles Preventing Investing
• Acknowledge the common mistakes to avoid.	• Business Checklist
• Decide which investments will help you achieve your financial goals.	• Fractional Ownership Benefits

Exercise 1

Choose three types of Fractional Ownership investments that you will focus on.

1. Investment A

2. Investment B

3. Investment C

Research specific companies in those investment areas and quickly glance over to determine which ones fit.

1. Business Name _____

Does the investment align with your values?	Yes	No
Do you lack knowledge about the industry?	Yes	No
Is it too complex that you need legal counsel?	Yes	No
Is it an illiquid and volatile asset or fund?	Yes	No
Is the company transparent in all aspects?	Yes	No

2. Business Name _____

Does the investment align with your values?	Yes	No
Do you lack knowledge about the industry?	Yes	No
Is it too complex that you need legal counsel?	Yes	No
Is it an illiquid and volatile asset or fund?	Yes	No
Is the company transparent in all aspects?	Yes	No

3. Business Name _____

Does the investment align with your values?	Yes	No
Do you lack knowledge about the industry?	Yes	No
Is it too complex that you need legal counsel?	Yes	No
Is it an illiquid and volatile asset or fund?	Yes	No
Is the company transparent in all aspects?	Yes	No

Exercise 2

Use one of the companies from above and use the Business Checklist to identify if this investment vehicle works for you more in-depth.

Business Name _____

- ☐ Which Risk Bucket   _____
- ☐ Shared Beliefs   Yes   No
- ☐ Owners   _____
- ☐ Past Business Experiences   _____
- ☐ Filter Out Sob Story   Yes   No
- ☐ How They Handle the Good and Bad Times _____
- ☐ Can They Dust Themselves Off if Told No   Yes   No
- ☐ Complicated or Simple Business Model (should be simple)   Yes   No
- ☐ Profit Model
- ☐ Revenue Model   _____
- ☐ Costs vs. Profit   _____
- ☐ Industry Lens   _____
- ☐ Financials   _____
- ☐ Marketing and Sales   _____
- ☐ New Funds   _____

Let's determine how you will fund the investment account.

- • Personal Savings _____
- • Accessible Credit _____
- • IRA/401K (self-directed) _____
- • Life Insurance _____
- • Funds from your Business _____

Now, deploy your funds and monitor the investment's progress.

- • Investment Name _____
- • Total Amount Invested _____
- • Date Invested _____
- • Maturity Date _____
- • Rate of Progress

Exercise 3

What are the benefits of each of the three types of Fractional Ownership investments you picked in **Exercise 1**?

1. Investment A _____

The risk level is acceptable and is easily accessible.	Yes	No
Is flexible enough for investors' customized needs.	Yes	No
It fits investors' purpose, beliefs, and goals.	Yes	No

2. Investment B _____

The risk level is acceptable and is easily accessible.	Yes	No
Is flexible enough for investors' customized needs.	Yes	No
It fits investors' purpose, beliefs, and goals.	Yes	No

3. Investment C _____

The risk level is acceptable and is easily accessible.	Yes	No
Is flexible enough for investors' customized needs.	Yes	No
It fits investors' purpose, beliefs, and goals.	Yes	No

You have a good idea about the investment types you're interested in and can see the benefits of Fractional Ownership investments. What about what you specifically picked in Exercise #2? Does it have more pros (benefits) than cons (obstacles)?

It will support diversification in my portfolio.	Yes	No
The company or person vetted is trustworthy.	Yes	No
It has a lower cost of entry.	Yes	No
It has excellent professional management techniques.	Yes	No
The anticipated ROI fits my needs.	Yes	No

Additional Notes:

CH7

Diversify Your Investments for Long-Term Success

Activation Prompt	Lessons from Chapter 7
• Attend workshops or webinars hosted by financial experts. • Create a mock investment portfolio to track while analyzing companies' financial statements. • Write an investment plan and review it regularly by staying up to date on market trends and news.	• Power of Diversification • Good Investor • Art and Science of Investing

Exercise 1

To empower yourself with a diversified portfolio, make a plan. Initial beside each commitment, then use the next page to help analyze if a workshop works for you.

I commit to:

- Setting realistic goals and regularly reviewing the progress towards these goals. _____

- Spending _____ hours each month studying the field of finances. _____

- Attending _____ workshops or webinars per month/year. _____

- Doing my due diligence before making any investment decisions. _____

- Hiring or closely following financial advisors that help keep me on track, such as: _____

  - _____

  - _____

  - _____

LIVE Financial Education Grid

Event Title	Speaker's Name	Date of Event	Event Website

What was the speaker's main point?	What is the speaker's background or expertise that leads to their credibility?

Filter out the bias, the stories, or any other means to sway an audience. List 3 arguments, data points, or case studies the speaker used as evidence.

-
-
-

Write two things you learned from this specific event, etc.

-
-

If you could ask the speaker a question, what would it be?	How would you implement the lessons and information learned into your personal financial strategy?	Who do you know would benefit from these lessons too?

Exercise 2

When using the Financial Decision Tree, you created your starting point, but now the plan is to turn you into a good investor with the lessons you've learned thus far.

1. Do you have an investment philosophy with a sound philosophy of diversification? Rate each of your investment values below on a scale of 0-10 to determine which of your values is least likely to be a value you will not break or bend to the most likely one you could never break or bend in your philosophy.

1	2	3	4	5	6	7	8	9	10
least likely									most likely

1	2	3	4	5	6	7	8	9	10
least likely									most likely

1	2	3	4	5	6	7	8	9	10
least likely									most likely

1	2	3	4	5	6	7	8	9	10
least likely									most likely

1	2	3	4	5	6	7	8	9	10
least likely									most likely

2. From the lists of investment types and companies you created in the previous exercises, does each one align with your values?   Yes   No

3. Do you have a good idea about risk buckets and have yours labeled and scaled from least to most important?   Yes   No

4. Are you prepared for when the market changes? Are you able to quickly review your buckets' importance to you or able to target other investments to stabilize the portfolio's financial performance?   Yes   No

5. Can you ensure you maintain a solid track record of returns to further your investments' longevity?   Yes   No

6. Have you used the RAD Keys and Business Checklist as part of your investment process criteria and added your nuanced factors to evaluate investments with?   Yes   No

7. Do you understand your money personality, the emotional triggers that may impact your investing, and do you have the strategies to manage your money personality strengths and weaknesses?   Yes   No

Exercise 3

Which criteria fall under the art or science of financial investing?

relies on the strategy created from quantitative and qualitative variables from a macroeconomic perspective	relies on mathematical models and metrics, detailed analysis of case studies data points

What is one aspect of the art of your investment plan?

I will study the current market trends and economic conditions that may impact the success of the investment strategy _____ per week/month/year.

I will follow key players in each alternative investment space, and study their track record and how they move. Starting with:

- Company Name _____ Asset Class _____
- Company Name _____ Asset Class _____
- Company Name _____ Asset Class _____

I will stay up-to-date on changing regulations and industry news that may impact my investments and adjust accordingly every _____ days.

What is one aspect of the science of your investment plan?

I will invest _____ per week/month/year.
I will review/track/adjust my investments every_____ days.

I have chosen the vehicles I will invest in and the risk bucket they fall into.

- Low-Risk
  - Low-Reward (name) _____
    - Asset Class   _____
    - Amount Invested   _____
    - Annual Performance Ratio   _____
    - Anticipated ROI   _____
    - Liquidity   _____
  - Moderate-Reward (name) _____
    - Asset Class   _____
    - Amount Invested   _____
    - Annual Performance Ratio   _____
    - Anticipated ROI   _____
    - Liquidity   _____
  - High-Reward (name) _____
    - Asset Class   _____
    - Amount Invested   _____
    - Annual Performance Ratio   _____
    - Anticipated ROI   _____
    - Liquidity   _____

- Moderate-Risk
  - Low-Reward (name) _____
    - Asset Class   _____
    - Amount Invested   _____
    - Annual Performance Ratio   _____
    - Anticipated ROI   _____
    - Liquidity   _____

- Moderate-Risk
  - Moderate-Reward (name) _____
    - Asset Class _____
    - Amount Invested _____
    - Annual Performance Ratio _____
    - Anticipated ROI _____
    - Liquidity _____
  - High-Reward (name) _____
    - Asset Class _____
    - Amount Invested _____
    - Annual Performance Ratio _____
    - Anticipated ROI _____
    - Liquidity _____

- High-Risk
  - Low-Reward (name) _____
    - Asset Class _____
    - Amount Invested _____
    - Annual Performance Ratio _____
    - Anticipated ROI _____
    - Liquidity _____
  - Moderate-Reward (name) _____
    - Asset Class _____
    - Amount Invested _____
    - Annual Performance Ratio _____
    - Anticipated ROI _____
    - Liquidity _____
  - High-Reward (name) _____
    - Asset Class _____
    - Amount Invested _____
    - Annual Performance Ratio _____
    - Anticipated ROI _____
    - Liquidity _____

Additional Notes:

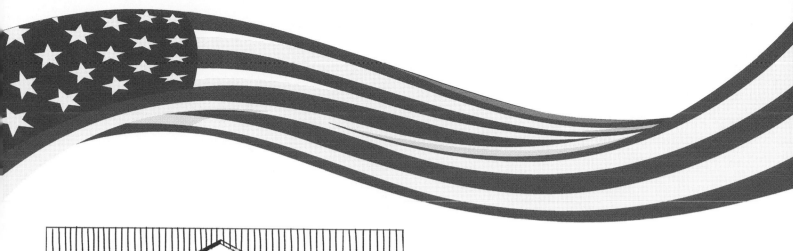

CH8

Leveraging Real Estate

Activation Prompt	Lessons from Chapter 8
• Analyze REITs and their potential for creating wealth and security.	• Keys to Real Estate Success
• List the risks and benefits associated with real estate investment properties.	• RADD's Diamond 5
• Identify the factors that affect the success of real estate investments.	• Common Real Estate Mistakes

Exercise 1

Analyze three REITs with the Keys to Real Estate Success and determine their potential to create wealth.

1. REIT A Name _____

   • Potential Benefits

     • _____
     • _____
     • _____

   • Potential Risks

     • _____
     • _____
     • _____

2. REIT B Name _____

   • Potential Benefits

     • _____
     • _____
     • _____

   • Potential Risks

     • _____
     • _____
     • _____

3. REIT C Name _____

   • Potential Benefits

     • _____
     • _____
     • _____

   • Potential Risks

     • _____
     • _____
     • _____

Exercise 2

Use the REITs you researched in Exercise #1, pick a property from each of their sites and analyze each one. Your analysis should follow a few of RADD's Diamond 5 principles to get started and then determine the potential risks and benefits investing in this property could create for your portfolio.

MLS sites like Zillow (**https://www.zillow.com/**), Realtor (**https://www.realtor.com/**), or even Roofstock (**https://www.roofstock.com/**) will help you analyze the properties more in-depth outside what the REITs provide. However, please note that these MLS sites offer estimations and are not always accurate or up-to-date information. They can give a rough ballpark number close enough to what the third-party vendors the REITs most likely used to evaluate their properties, and it provides an idea of the market trends.

1. REIT A Name

   Property Address: City, State:

   _____   _____

   Purchase Price: Sold (if so, at what price):

   _____   _____

   Associated Fees (like HOA):   Value-Add Features (repairs + more):

   _____   _____

   _____   _____

   _____   _____

   - Thrive During Economic Hardships:

     - Project Type: Rental, Flip, Other

     - Debt-to-Equity Ratio: Low   High

     - Favorable Risk-Return Profile: Yes   No

   - Compound Acceleration:

     - Long-Term Lease Agreements: Yes   No

     - Positive Rental Growth Trends: Yes   No

     - Favorable Interest Rates: Yes   No

- Profit Strategy:

    - Value-Add Opportunities: Yes   No

    - Team's Market Expertise: Yes   No

    - Capital Allocation Strategy: _____

- Location, Location, Location:

    - Desirable Neighborhoods: Grade

    - Access to Transportation and/or Hospital: Yes   No

    - Population Growth: _____ %

- Alternative Investments:

    - Environmental, Social, Governance (ESG)   _____

                                                 _____

                                                 _____

    - Growing Investor Demand   Yes   No

    - Potential Tax Benefits   _____

- Social Impact Investments:

    - Long-Term Appreciation Potential   Yes   No

    - Hedge Against Inflation   Yes   No

    - Social and Environmental Benefits   _____

Will it be ideal to invest in the REIT with your analysis of this property?

_____

_____

2. REIT B Name _____

Property Address: _____   City, State: _____

_____   _____

Purchase Price: _____   Sold (if so, at what price): _____

_____   _____

Associated Fees (like HOA):   Value-Add Features (repairs + more):

_____   _____

_____   _____

_____   _____

_____   _____

- Thrive During Economic Hardships:

  - Project Type: Rental, Flip, Other

  - Debt-to-Equity Ratio: Low   High

  - Favorable Risk-Return Profile: Yes   No

- Compound Acceleration:

  - Long-Term Lease Agreements: Yes   No

  - Positive Rental Growth Trends: Yes   No

  - Favorable Interest Rates: Yes   No

- Profit Strategy:

  - Value-Add Opportunities: Yes   No

  - Team's Market Expertise: Yes   No

  - Capital Allocation Strategy: _____

- Location, Location, Location:
  - Desirable Neighborhoods: Grade _____
  - Access to Transportation and/or Hospital: Yes   No
    - Population Growth: _____ %

  - Alternative Investments:
    - Environmental, Social, Governance (ESG)   _____

                         _____

    - Growing Investor Demand   Yes   No
    - Potential Tax Benefits   _____
  - Social Impact Investments:
    - Long-Term Appreciation Potential   Yes   No
    - Hedge Against Inflation   Yes   No
    - Social and Environmental Benefits   _____

Will it be ideal to invest in the REIT with your analysis of this property?

_____

3. REIT C Name _____

Property Address: City, State:

_____   _____

Purchase Price: Sold (if so, at what price):

_____   _____

Associated Fees (like HOA):   Value-Add Features (repairs + more):

_____   _____

_____   _____

_____   _____

_____   _____

- Thrive During Economic Hardships:

  - Project Type: Rental, Flip, Other

  - Debt-to-Equity Ratio: Low   High

  - Favorable Risk-Return Profile: Yes   No

- Compound Acceleration:

  - Long-Term Lease Agreements: Yes   No

  - Positive Rental Growth Trends: Yes   No

  - Favorable Interest Rates: Yes   No

- Profit Strategy:

  - Value-Add Opportunities: Yes   No

  - Team's Market Expertise: Yes   No

  - Capital Allocation Strategy: _____

- Location, Location, Location:

  - Desirable Neighborhoods.   Grade _____

  - Access to Transportation and/or Hospital: Yes   No

  - Population Growth: _____ %

- Alternative Investments:

  - Environmental, Social, Governance (ESG)   _____

                                            _____

                                            _____

  - Growing Investor Demand   Yes   No

  - Potential Tax Benefits

- Social Impact Investments:

    - Long-Term Appreciation Potential   Yes   No

    - Hedge Against Inflation   Yes   No

    - Social and Environmental Benefits   _____

Will it be ideal to invest in the REIT with your analysis of this property?

_____

Exercise 3

There are factors that affect the success or failure of a REIT. Choose those factors that you weigh heaviest in your decision-making. Rank them in order of importance if that helps you too.

☐ Type of Real Estate and Diversification   _____

☐ Location of Real Estate   _____

☐ Market and Economic Conditions   _____

☐ Company/Management/Owner   _____

☐ Past Performance of REIT   _____

☐ Past Performance of Company/Management/Owner   _____

☐ Financial Strength of the REIT   _____

Consider those factors you've ranked, and further analyze the REITs you researched in the previous exercises according to the 10 Common Real Estate Mistakes. Determine which REITs have the least amount of mistakes, and how that may be an example of a stable business model.

Categories	REIT A		REIT B		REIT C	
Following the herd and buying retail.	Yes	No	Yes	No	Yes	No
Buying because there's new development.	Yes	No	Yes	No	Yes	No
Avoid the unicorn.	Yes	No	Yes	No	Yes	No
Giving your money to someone with no experience.	Yes	No	Yes	No	Yes	No
Investing just because someone you know is.	Yes	No	Yes	No	Yes	No
Trusting the due diligence of others.	Yes	No	Yes	No	Yes	No
Buying for the short-term.	Yes	No	Yes	No	Yes	No
Buying virtually without a plan.	Yes	No	Yes	No	Yes	No
Buying the cheapest real estate.	Yes	No	Yes	No	Yes	No
Using unlicensed or cheap contractors.	Yes	No	Yes	No	Yes	No

Total Mistakes: _____ _____ _____

Additional Notes:

CH9

Leveraging Real Estate

Activation Prompt	Lessons from Chapter 9
• Analyze tax regulations and how they currently or will affect you. • Identify which regulations can protect your assets or eliminate taxes. • Strategize which ones can feasibly support you now and plan how to utilize other codes in the future.	• Tax Codes and Regulations • Tax Circle • Tax Strategy

Exercise 1

By testing your knowledge of tax regulations, you will gain a better understanding of how to optimize your investments and take advantage of any available tax benefits. Then analyze your current situation and how it may affect your goals.

1. What is the current standard deduction for a single taxpayer? Am I investing in a tax-efficient manner through deductions, retirement accounts, or investments?

_____

_____

_____

_____

_____

_____

_____

2. How does the capital gains tax rate differ for short-term and long-term investments? Analyze how changes in tax rates could impact the after-tax returns of a taxable investment portfolio.

_____

_____

_____

_____

_____

_____

_____

3. Are there any future tax law changes that could impact my investments? How might these changes impact my financial strategy and goals?

_____

_____

_____

_____

_____

_____

_____

_____

Exercise 2

Pick three of any investment you researched in the previous chapter exercises to see how the tax regulations you researched in Exercise #1 will protect them or increase your tax deduction amounts. Use the Tax Circle to help you picture how your money will move towards each step.

1. Investment Type A _____ _____

☐ Percentage of Income		_____ %
☐ Utilizing Debt	Yes	No
☐ Rate of Returns	Low	High
☐ Cycling Returns	Yes	No
☐ Management Fees that affect Returns	Yes	No
☐ Insurance on Investments	Yes	No
☐ Using a Business Structure (LLC, etc.)	Yes	No
☐ Using 1031s, Opportunity Zones, or IRAs/401(k)s	Yes	No
☐ Market Demand	Low	High
☐ Correlation to Traditional Asset Classes	Low	High

2. Investment Type B _____

☐ Percentage of Income	_____ %	
☐ Utilizing Debt	Yes	No
☐ Rate of Returns	Low	High
☐ Cycling Returns	Yes	No
☐ Management Fees that affect Returns	Yes	No
☐ Insurance on Investments	Yes	No
☐ Using a Business Structure (LLC, etc.)	Yes	No
☐ Using 1031s, Opportunity Zones, or IRAs/401(k)s	Yes	No
☐ Market Demand	Low	High
☐ Correlation to Traditional Asset Classes	Low	High

3. Investment Type C _____

☐ Percentage of Income	_____ %	
☐ Utilizing Debt	Yes	No
☐ Rate of Returns	Low	High
☐ Cycling Returns	Yes	No
☐ Management Fees that affect Returns	Yes	No
☐ Insurance on Investments	Yes	No
☐ Using a Business Structure (LLC, etc.)	Yes	No
☐ Using 1031s, Opportunity Zones, or IRAs/401(k)s	Yes	No
☐ Market Demand	Low	High
☐ Correlation to Traditional Asset Classes	Low	High

Exercise 3

Consider where you are falling short for your financial plan, based on your answers in the previous exercises, and consider the next steps to turn it into the most efficient action you can take. This will mean implementing a tax strategy to make your investments more productive.

Go through the list below, and make a few final decisions or start researching more where you left off with a few investments to make them work for you.

1. A Team with an Educator Mindset
- Business_____ Website _____
- Business_____ Website _____
- Business_____ Website _____

2. 1031 Exchanges
- Business_____ Website _____
- Business_____ Website _____
- Business_____ Website

3. Opportunity Zones
- Business_____ Website _____
- Business_____ Website _____
- Business_____ Website _____

4. Retirement Plans
- Business_____ Website _____
- Business_____ Website _____
- Business_____ Website _____

5. Legal Counsel
- Business_____ Website _____
- Business_____ Website _____
- Business_____ Website _____

6. Asset Protection
- Business_____ Website _____
- Business_____ Website _____
- Business_____ Website _____

7. Investment Design

Consider your top investment choices as you briefly differentiate how they diversify your portfolio and where they are in the Tax Circle to help determine the next steps.

- Investment _____   Asset Class _____
- Rate of Returns _____   Shelter _____
- Risk Bucket _____   Tax Efficiency _____

  Need more research time or professional guidance to dive into it deeper?

- Investment _____   Asset Class _____
- Rate of Returns _____   Shelter _____
- Risk Bucket _____   Tax Efficiency _____

  Need more research time or professional guidance to dive into it deeper?

- Investment _____   Asset Class _____
- Rate of Returns _____   Shelter _____
- Risk Bucket _____   Tax Efficiency _____

  Need more research time or professional guidance to dive into it deeper?

Additional Notes:

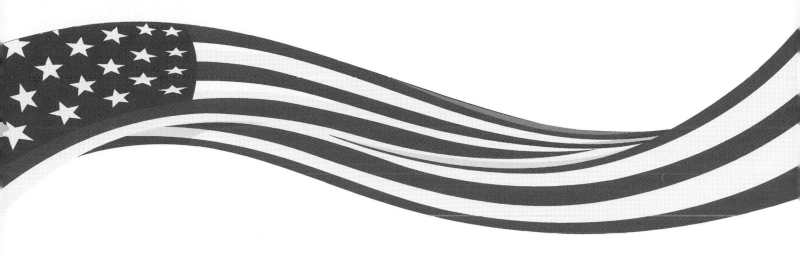

CH10

Building Your Legacy and Making a Positive Impact

Activation Prompt	Lessons from Chapter 10
• Discuss different tactics to educate family members, including children or grandchildren. • Identify the key components of estate planning and why it is important to transfer wealth. • Understand how your personal journey of growth and self-discovery is making an impact.	• Educating Children • Estate Planning • Legacy Planning

Exercise 1

How can you teach a child, of any age, how to plan for their financial freedom and achieve their dreams? It probably starts with the simple things that you can bring up in daily conversations, or can help weekly reinforce their motivations and staying on target.

- ☐ Allowance management and teach your child how to manage saving, spending, and giving.

- ☐ Practice delayed gratification and set savings goals if there's something your child really wants to buy.

- ☐ Get your children involved in financial decisions, such as choosing a grocery store and comparing prices of items, or even in the process of your financial plans like debt management, investment education, and tax strategies.

- ☐ Create a budget with money buckets and teach your child how to make money work through income, living costs, and investing.

- ☐ If your child is slightly older, and start teaching them money personalities, how they change over time, and train them how to utilize their strengths and weaknesses.

Games are another fabulous way of educating children. The teach how to save, the importance of investing, and the consequences of poor financial decision-making. Depending on the age of the child, consider which game would be the best fit.

- ☐ Monopoly for Kids (ages 4-7)

- ☐ Classic Monopoly (ages 8 and over)

- ☐ CashFlow for Kids (ages 6-10)

- ☐ Financial Peace Jr. (ages 3-12)

- ☐ Black Millionaires of Tomorrow

Financial Education Game Time (create your routine)

Weekly on _____ at _____ am/pm.

Monthly _____ (Example: the first Saturday at 7 pm).

As kids get older, it might be great to dive deeper in how they prep for their future. Teach them the following on how it works, how it will help them save money, and how they can use compounding strategies to make money work for them to achieve their own goals.

- ☐ Interest and Credit
- ☐ Taxes and Regulations
- ☐ Alternative Investments
- ☐ Due Diligence
- ☐ Financial Decision Tree

All of this material can also be a conversation you bring up with adult family and friends when they specifically request support.

Exercise 2

An Effective Estate Plan Includes (make sure to consult with an attorney or qualified professional):

- Will:
  - Appoint an Executor
  - Designate Beneficiaries
  - Identify Assets to be Distributed
- Living Revocable Trust:
  - Identify a Trustee
  - Designate Beneficiaries
  - Transfer Assets and Establish Terms
- Durable Power of Attorney:
  - Appoint an Agent
  - Define Scope of Authority
  - Specify Limitations and Establish Duration
- Living Will:
  - Specify End-of-Life Medical Treatment Preferences
  - Instructions for Organ and Tissue Donation
  - Appoint a Healthcare Agent
- Health Care Surrogacy:
  - Designate a Surrogate Decision-Maker for Medical Treatment
  - Specify if Decision-Making Authority is Broad or Limited in Scope
  - Instructions for Surrogate Decision-Maker Regarding Personal Wishes

Exercise 3

Breaking free from your "Money Shackles" positions you to build real wealth. Creating a legacy involves a serious plan of how you will pass on your wealth and influence in the way you choose.

Education

_____ I will provide my spouse, children and grandchildren with a thorough education on building and maintaining wealth.

Money

$_____ for my spouse

$_____ for each of my children

$_____ for each of my grandchildren

$_____ for other beneficiaries

$_____ for Charities

    Charity Name _____ # _____

    Charity Name _____ # _____

    Charity Name _____ # _____

Real Estate

My personal home left to _____

My rental properties left to _____

Stocks/Bonds/Mutual Funds left to _____

Alternative Investments left to _____

IRA/401K(s) left to _____

Additional Notes:

Unlocking Your Financial Potential

Activation Prompt	Lessons from Chapter 1
• How will you overcome potential barriers while staying committed? • Review and establish steps to become a great investor. • Act on your new financial plan to your Redefined American Dream.	• Overcoming Barriers • Great Investor • Financial Movement

Exercise 1

I completely understand that my journey to financial freedom will require persistence, tenacity, and patience.

There will be barriers to overcome, but I can break the "Money Shackles" and circumvent the "Freedom Traps" that will try to overwhelm me and change my course of action.

To prevent this, I will reinforce my "Mindset" regularly (check each one you can do).

- ☐ Assess and adjust financial plans and dreams for lasting impact.

- ☐ Read and study financial principles, and understand how my money personality may react or change when implementing them.

- ☐ Avoid negative influences (media, groups, individuals) and follow reliable sources for information related to my investing.

- ☐ Diversify my investment portfolio with alternative investments, and become a Fractional Owner.

- ☐ Manage investment risks with money buckets while leveraging borrowing and compound interest.

- ☐ Navigate tax codes and regulations with a team, and understand cycles in the market along with anomalies (COVID-19) that can impact ROI.

- ☐ Build and protect long-term investments to ensure my purpose, legacy, and impact have a positive effect.

Exercise 2

Steps to becoming a GREAT INVESTOR (write an action plan for each one):

1. Know what your Redefined American Dream goals are, and the investment philosophy that will help you achieve it, even if or when the dream changes. Know it inside and out, its strengths and weaknesses, and determine your investment design strategy will be a lot quicker.

_____

_____

_____

2. Make a commitment to the process required to become a great investor, i.e. following the Financial Decision Tree, reading financial news, or listening to podcasts. Set a daily or weekly schedule to review critical and reliable information.

_____

_____

_____

3. Schedule at least two major financial workshops, seminars, or webinars annually. Sign up, and book your accommodations and airfare (if needed). Consider VIP status to network with those with a higher financial IQ, and/or joining a mastermind or group like our "Inner Circle."

_____

_____

_____

4. Create a spreadsheet, or something similar, to track your portfolio and monitor your diversification across asset classes, industries, and ESG considerations. Engage in impact investing that aligns with your values and have a positive impact. Set a monthly or quarterly schedule to regularly rebalance your portfolio to maintain diversification.

_____

_____

_____

5. Use historical data with the art and science of investing parameters, to simulate potential investment outcomes based on different scenarios and market conditions. Use this information to inform your decision-making and take calculated risks before the market changes, not after.

_____

_____

_____

6. Hire a financial coach to assist you with accountability. Build a team. Choose professionals who can help and educate you navigate complex financial issues, including tax codes and regulations, legal issues, and investment strategies.

_____

_____

_____

7. Mentor others with less financial education than you and to network to gain new insights. Build a community of support. You'll grow exponentially when you do.

_____

_____

_____

Exercise 3

You have completed the chapter exercises of the book Money Shackles: The Breakout Guide to Alternative Investing. You're on your way to creating or pushing your Redefined American Dream forward.

What can you do immediately to have these lessons take effect for your journey?

Actions I can take:

Buy 3 Books on Finances (digital, physical, audio)   _____

Search for at least 1 Financial Training and Book It   _____

Hire a Financial Coach   _____

Join a Group like Inner Circle or MasterMind   _____

Commit to Mentoring 1 Other Person   _____

Schedule 1+ Hour/Week to Financial Education   _____

Schedule 1+ Hour/Week to Develop your Growth Mindset   _____

Have you created a vision board before? If you've never created a vision board before, consider the following resources:

- Science (**https://www.scienceofpeople.com/how-to-make-a-vision-board/**)
- Canva (**https://www.canva.com/create/vision-boards/**)
- TedTalk (**https://www.youtube.com/watch?v=KiWrMUek2cU**)

Reflect on the most influential exercises from this workbook that have helped you with your journey thus far. In a few words write their lessons and sketch out your own vision board for your Redefined American Dream below.

Knowing where you are, where you are going, and how you accomplish it will help you make massive actionable strides now that you have a good foundation.

Share your financial journey with others. Mentoring others will help you grow. Encourage others to join a financial movement towards achieving their own financial freedom and Redefined American Dream.

Additional Notes:

Additional Notes:

Additional Notes:

Additional Notes:

Additional Notes:

About the Author and RAD Diversified

Dutch Mendenhall, the founder of RAD Diversified, is a pioneer of innovation and growth within the American Dream. With over 15 years of experience in real estate and education, Mendenhall has demonstrated his expertise and authority as a Thought Leader in the industry. Moreover, his personal experiences have contributed to his success, as reflected in his work with RAD Diversified.

TheRAD™, the educational entity of RAD Diversified, addresses crucial issues such as empowering individuals to Redefine their American Dream through smart investing and diversification. It is designed for anyone seeking to leverage their wealth to create positive social change and achieve financial freedom. The program aims to empower individuals and families to secure a prosperous future through the strength of real estate investments, done right and done together. Whether someone is looking to improve their financial situation, struggling with debt, or interested in alternative investment methods and diversification strategies, TheRAD™ is the gateway to a better future.

Dutch Mendenhall and his team thrive on facing the challenges in today's society and market. They aim to make a difference in people's lives, so they prioritize taking action and educating themselves on a variety of industries and investment strategies that keep them ahead as market leaders. They make informed decisions and transform their lifestyle to continue putting them in positions to succeed. This approach has helped them build the RAD Diversified brand, which thrives and serves the community of investors they work with and care about.

For Mendenhall and his team, empowering others with financial knowledge and creating a community of like-minded individuals who support each other's goals is crucial. They believe in fostering strong relationships based on trust, transparency, and accountability. This approach has helped them build a Tribe invested in each other's success.

Their dedication to education, community-building, and transformative investment strategies sets Mendenhall and his team apart. Their commitment to positively impacting people's lives and creating a legacy of financial empowerment for future generations is unprecedented in today's "Get Mine" wealth-building environment. Their philosophy proves to be a separator between them and the rest of the industry.

When analyzing the meaning of the American Dream from history to the present day, it becomes clear that innovation and growth are key factors in achieving success. Dutch Mendenhall has the knowledge and skills to address these issues and jump-start a revolutionary financial movement. His approach has been proven effective through case studies and real-world examples.

Implementing Mendenhall's solutions involves putting the relevant lessons learned to the test against traditional thinking and powerful economic waves. With his expertise and that of his team, they have the ability to make an impact on the industry never seen before. Mendenhall's approach prioritizes financial education, community building, and transformative investment strategies that empower investors to break free from financial limitations and achieve their goals.

Overall, the RADD team's dedication to innovation, growth, expertise, and experience make them a viable option for those looking to achieve financial success and transform their lives. Their practical and effective solutions make them a valuable resource for anyone looking to break free from financial limitations and achieve their idea of the American Dream.

Redefining the American Dream with new mindsets and leveraging traditional values can lead to success. This book explores the impact of implementing the tips, techniques, and lessons learned from this book. It will give you the tools to create the plan that turns your life into your American Dream.

Dutch Mendenhall and "TheRAD" lead the way toward a brighter future for all Americans. Addressing the wealth crisis and promoting innovation and growth paved the way for everyone to unlock their vision for their future. The story is not over, but together, we can achieve the new American Dream with the right mindset and actions.

WEBSITES

RAD Diversified REIT
(https://raddiversified.com/)

RADD Inner Circle
(https://icradd.com/)

RADD America
(https://raddamerica.com/)

TheRAD
(https://therad.com/)

The RADD Podcast
(https://www.theraddpodcast.com/)

Download the Money
Shackles Workbook PDF